By the people, For the people.

A story.

by
sascha benjamin cohen

(This fable, originally written in 2011, has been updated and corrected to align with the new normal as we approach 2024).

ARTICLE I. Beginning 90 days from the ratification of this amendment, elections shall cease to be the operative method for the selection of Executive and Legislative Branches of the federal government of the United States. Those individuals formerly identified therein as Electors, will be known hereafter as Selectors.

On October 18th, the day the 35th amendment to the US constitution was ratified, 11,000 cases of champagne were consumed. 300 parades were organized between the borders of Oregon in the West, and Tennessee in the East. 14,089 births were recorded in the 51 states. 6,953 deaths occurred between sunrise and sunset. Of those deaths, 87 were eventually recorded as homicides, eleven of them accidental, fourteen spousal acts of passion. There were four dozen significant house fires, three of them arson; there were four actions later classified as terrorism, three of those led by white supremacist groups with strong secessionist leanings and ties to the Maga underground; the other by Marvin Walsh, a recently laid-off aeronautics maintenance worker with a history of mental illness. There were no significant class action suits filed, and not a single tornado was recorded on US territory.

And that night, just past midnight, in a small hospital on the California coast, the future first-in-*minyan* of the Pork Bun Jews was born.

After the civil unrest of the Bad Years, the move to clarify and simplify the nest of rules that governed our lives grew greater and greater. The early war movements --- the Tea Party, the Progressive Caucus, the post-Maga, neo-trumpists and the White Lighters, the movements to revoke the 17th and 24th amendments, the groups demanding the abolition of the Electoral College --- particularly after the bitterly disputed elections of 2028 --- along with the perennial rabble of confederate daydreamers, creationists, Klan sympathizers, socialists, isolationists, flat taxers, libertarians, universal health care nuts, climate change denialists, and even the old Trumpite sect after their savior's purported apotheosis --- with the lack of center, all the outliers and fringes began to coalesce, and find common ground. And honestly, who wouldn't prefer something simpler and more honest than the divisive mess that our elections had become? Owned by the oligarchy, drummed by purchased polls, devoid of any real value for the common folk; after the long years of battles abroad, and the fights here at home, and the death and loss it had brought, our elections were just another glaring example of what was wrong with our world, and the poor choices we had made. And what poor choices those had been! God, it hurts to even be reminded now. Honestly: who wants to be faced with their mistakes? Where is the profit in *that*?

When the minority whip in Congress bought an hour of time across the media, and made the stunning suggestion that it was less important to *elect* our leaders than it was to make sure that those leaders were truly *selected* from among The People --- and in turn, that the people could track instantly and immediately their approval or distaste with the actions that those leaders take, and the words they speak, and the personal proclivities that the press are able to uncover in the course of their work --- something about the suggestion, and the way his eyes sparkled on every 3DHD screen across the nation, and the lilt in his soothing voice, well: it just clicked. And the movement was on.

> ***ARTICLE II. Election shall be replaced with a random selection lottery, containing the name of every mentally competent citizen who has reached the age of 30. The lottery will be governed by the Selectors of the States, who will continue to convene to oversee and verify the lottery activities. The lottery will be comprised of two processes of Selection: First, the selection of citizens for service, and Second, the matching of those citizens to offices of government.***
>
> ***ARTICLE III. This amendment supersedes all defining matter regarding election of governmental office in this constitution, in particular Article 1, Sections 2 and 4; Article 2, Section 1; the 12th amendment and all electoral determinations to which it pertains; the 17th amendment and all electoral determinations to which it pertains, the 20th amendment and all electoral determinations to which it pertains; the 22nd amendment and all electoral determinations to which it pertains; 24th amendment and all electoral determinations to which it pertains.***

What a relief for the nation! In one fell swoop, we altered so many of our ills: eliminating the terror of the election cycle, we could focus on what we wanted as a nation, rather than who. With the end of elections, it also meant an end to campaigning, and an end to the unbound costs of that disastrous battle. In under five years, the billions of dollars that were previously spent on elections were being funneled back into our once ailing economy, providing the basis for the renewal of the post-war period. And suddenly, for the first time in decades, even an ordinary man or woman on the street could understand the law of the land, in simple easy terms. Even someone like me, with only a single post-graduate degree, and a 6.5 grade point average, could make sense of constitutional law. Now I could chime in online, and be heard, just as easily as a lawyer with the typical half-dozen university degrees and 8.0 GPA in their past, and have just as much authority over the text. Further, once congress had enshrined textual literalism and originalism as law, and interpretation was tossed out as a muddy and immoral activity, it was truly possible for everyone to feel as though they truly understood the law, and could make a choice as to whether or not it was right for them.

The first cycle of Selection was messy, of course, but once the draft letters started going out, people got into the spirit of it. And once we all received our LiveWire LikeIt!® paddles, allowing us to give a thumbs up (or thumbs down), in real time, to any word or action of any Selected Official in government, and to have that immediately posted to the online polls for the entire nation to see, well, that was when things really took off.

Greetings.

You have been selected at random, according to constitutional law, to serve in the next cycle of Government Service. You must respond to this letter within 15 calendar days by contacting your local FedGov office (appointments can be made at https://fedgov.gov/selected). Not responding is a federal crime, and punishable by fine, imprisonment, or both (fed. civ. code 923-1A.302.622-f).

Your Selection Number is ***#9800078402104573****. Please use it in all communications with your Selection officials.*

Upon contacting your local FedGov office, you will be informed of the process for induction and preparation, and will be given all the necessary information and training for your service. As determined by Congress, salary for your Selection cycle will be $65,000.00 per year, exclusive of health care and other standard benefits as described in government pamphlet HR-980v. Law prohibits the addition to that salary from any source, by any means, until the term of your service is complete. If you have income from other sources, it will be held for you in blind trust for *the duration of your service.*

For this cycle, you have been drawn in the pool for the following branch of Government:

Executive

In order to begin your service, and to verify your identity and receipt of this letter, please use the following contacts [....]

Congratulations, and welcome to Selected Service,

Lou Valenti,

Deputy Assistant Secretary of Selection Services

When I got my first letter, I was 34 years old. I was living on Pacific, in a walk-up one bedroom at the edge of Chinatown which I'd been in since my divorce. Work had been slow that year, and while I was making rent and paying the bills, I hadn't had a lot of free cash. Then again, contract plumbing isn't exactly a glamorous profession. But since I'd never finished my second PhD, there weren't a lot of career choices open to me, and I'd always been pretty good with my hands. I almost missed the letter; I don't pay too much attention to the snail mail, since I'm not a big coupon fan. But it was a heavy stiff envelope, and when I dropped it on the table it made a thud I felt more than heard. And there it was: with the embossed official seal of the government on the front.

My first thought was what a damned bad time it was to receive a selection summons: my savings were pretty shot, and the thought of having to rebuild clientele after years away in Washington seemed like a purgatory for the damned. But there it was, like I said. A solid reminder of my country, and the sad fact that unlike most of my friends and acquaintances, I actually have moral qualms about not following the law.

So what did I do? Well, first things first: I sure didn't call the feds. I picked up the phone, and punched up my buddy from the *minyan*, Joseph.

"Yeah, what?"

"Hi Joe."

"Yeah, I'm kinda busy right now, Maury. What is it?"

"Busy? With what?"

Silence. Then, in a stage whisper

"I'm fucking a co-ed shiksa, if you must know." There was a stifled giggle in the background.

"Right now?"

“Nearly. And this call is interrupting my game.”

“Is her name Thumbelina Myhand?”

“Shut up, asshole. What do you want?”

“I just got a letter from the Selector Service.”

“Maury, no shit?”

“Yeah. I’m staring at the letter right now. Got it in my hand. Official seal and everything.”

“Hot damn. Listen, let me explain to Judy, and I’ll be over in ten.”

“Judy? You’re banging Judy Kleinman?”

“Well, I’m trying. But clearly I’m not having the best of luck right at the moment. I’ll see you in ten, OK?”

“OK.”

I should explain something about the *minyan*. It was a year or two after school, and a few of my friends had been meeting up most weekend mornings for a brunch, political bitch session, and general socializing. And yes, we were (are) all Jews, or at least jew-ish. Not black hats, but all with family that pushed us to remember our tribal roots. All of us remembered; none of us joined up with the team. Oh, we all knew where the nearest synagogue was, and probably could recite all the daily prayers from childhood memory, if someone pointed a gun to our heads. But we weren't of the faithful. Or even of the social community. We were a gaggle of awkward post-graduates with a penchant for chatter and dim sum on Sundays. So we decided to amuse ourselves by forming a collective, something that would fly in the face of established religion, piss off our parents and relatives, and generally give us an excuse to act out. And the *minyan* of the Pork Bun Jews of Pacific Street was born.

Every Sunday, a table for ten at Tree Hugger Dim Sum (all organic! all the time!), and we'd banter, cajole, demean and embarrass one another, in the subconscious hope of replacing the familial and spiritual communities we had abandoned with something we could understand, that would fill the ever-expanding void. Joseph, Craig, Sally, Laura Campanelli, Isaac, Nadav, Lila and Juha, David (Joe's little brother), and me: Maury Andritch, first-in-minyan by general consensus (and since it was my idea in the first place). Joe was my best friend; I knew Craig and Sally through him. Laura Campanelli had some time ago outgrown the teen shaming misogynist title once given to her by the jock & skirt claque of McKinley High (don't ask -- it's a sore point) to become my former wife. Isaac and Nadav we knew from undergrad days at Cal. They had met while working on the Rainbow Gazette --- Isaac as art director and Nadav as general editor --- and had been together ever since. Lila and Juha were twins, they had moved into the neighborhood at some point and made themselves known by being far and away the strangest yet most disturbingly charismatic personalities in the district.

What kept us together? Sharp intellects, shared appreciations, mutual disavowal of the families and who had raised us and the traditions they inculcated us with. We were friends with a penchant for irony, for the bitter and the absurd. And a good pork bun never hurt.

That, of course, was years ago. They are all dead now, unmourned and unremembered. Except for me.

The door buzzer went off. I looked at the security monitor, and saw Joe's long profile. "Dude." I buzzed him in.

Joe was teaching general history at a local community college. He loved his job, but he loved his female students more. "The way I see it," he said to me, "I can either get laid or get tenure. And I think I am going to opt for getting laid. At least until someone demands I publish something meatier than I have so far, or I get slammed with a restraining order. Or a paternity suit. Or both." Joe had a simple if deeply offensive approach to life; I liked him for that. He was understandable.

As he walked in the door, I handed him my summons. He looked at it, and then looked at me. "Holy shit. Do you know what this means?"

"Yeah. It means I've got a royal pain in my plumber's ass."

"Maury, you idiot: you will never have to fix a broken toilet again. Don't you understand? No one just stops when they are done in office; you are a politician for four years, maybe six; but you're a celebrity for ever after amen. You've got policy think tanks after you, lecture circuits, product placements, guest spots on sitcoms, you name it! You won't have time to work on leaky pipes, even if you wanted to. And what's more, did you *look* at this letter?"

"Sure, I looked at it. Why the hell do you think I called you?"

"No, you bonehead. I mean really looked. What branch of government did you get called up for?"

"Huh? Whatever it says. Executive, right?"

Joe heaved a sigh heavy with exasperation. "Dammit,

how many letters do you think go out for Executive Branch Selection each cycle?"

And suddenly, it started to sink in.... "Oh shit. Shit shit shit shit *shit*!"

Dude, that's right. You're going to be President."

ARTICLE IV. This amendment in no way alters the duties, oaths, or exigencies of the offices to be selected; it confirms all terms of service, all chains of command, and any other attributes of office which are defined and designated elsewhere in this constitution, including those outlined in the 22nd amendment of this constitution. Should an individual be selected in a manner conflicting with these, a public notification of such will be made, and the name will be removed from that selection cycle for the office in question.

"...Or Vice President."

Joe shrugged. "Same diff. You're in the White House, dude. You're not just Mr. Nobody from Buttfuck Junction heading up to be a representative in the House. You're going to be in the spotlight, leading the country for the next four years!"

As he spoke, I began to experience strange tunnel vision, and was suddenly acutely aware of the air against my skin. Joe went on, now pacing around my living room, waving my summons like a fan in front of him.

"You will be in demand for the rest of your life, Maury! You are about to enter the realm of celebrity. And christ---what did you make in your best year as a friggin' plumber? 250? 275?"

I looked at him. "280."

"And do you know what former presidents make on the open market? Last I heard, President Mueller was pulling down 20 million, just from his book contracts and his spot with Coca-Cola. This, my friend, is your golden ticket." He stopped his peripatetic motion, and stared at me. "Man, this is going to be *so cool*!"

LikeIt!®

"While it now seems inevitable, the confluence of popular culture, direct democracy, and the advancement of technology to promote the process of government was not immediately obvious to anyone when the 35th amendment was proposed. It was only through the process of approval, and the refinement of its implementation that it became clear not only how significant an improvement it made over existing procedure, but also how remarkable a tool it would become for the clarification of the rules which govern our behavior. The ability to provide direct, interactive feedback for officeholders, along with the entertainment value of that feedback and its outcomes, has now provided the United States with a form of government envied by the rest of the civilized world."

(-From the Wikipedia entry on "Government Selection Service", edit 300 v.2)

"Any previous leadership experience? Organizing? Union stuff? Anything?" Colonel Valenti looked at me from heavy-lidded eyes, and then focused back on the forms lying between his hands on the desk.

"Well, not really..."

"Not really? Does that mean, 'sort of', or 'not at all'? Listen, Mr. Andritch, this isn't the time to be shy, or self-deprecating. I need everything from you that there is, so we can build a program that will make you the most effective citizen leader possible. Do you understand?"

A small nod from me.

"Good. So: any leadership experience?"

"Well, I helped organize a letter writing campaign for the Student Union back in grad school, years ago. But it didn't really go too well."

Actually, it had collapsed emphatically under its own pathetic weight. We got out four letters from the two recruits I was able to drag in, and none of them got sent. But Joe wound up dating one of them for a remarkable eleven weeks, during which he did not seduce nor was he seduced by a single undergraduate.

"Hmmm." Valenti had the thoughtful, under the breath "*hmmm*" perfected. It was a pinnacle of artistic mastery with him.

"I also host a brunch." Valenti looked up.

"Tell me more."

"It's a once a month thing: we get together and eat and talk politics and philosophy. It's a pretty eclectic group."

"Hmmm. And you lead this group? Keep it going, select discussion topics, order the bagels?"

"Yeah, I guess so. It's actually not bagels, though. It's dim sum."

"Hmmm." Another note on the form.

"But we are a *minyan.*"

This is awarded another heavy lidded 'you-must-be-screwing-with-me-kid' look. I can understand that it must be a taxing job, being in the career civil service and heading up a department that has to manage people like me, just in order to make sure we keep having a government. But he doesn't have to be quite so abrasive. At least, that is what I thought then. "Continue."

"We are a minyan, a group of ten Jews who form the minimum number to qualify as a community for praying together. But we don't pray; we just eat dim sum."

"And talk politics."

"Right. We all live in the same neighborhood, too, so we call ourselves the Pork Bun Jews of Pacific Street."

Valenti gives out a championship *hmmmm* and puts

his pen down, his hands moving together delicately in front of him, fingertips just touching as if to generate some infinitesimal arc of human energy between their pads. “This is going to be a big winner with the public. Some Jewish kid from San Francisco who eats Chinese pastries and unclogs toilets is somehow going to inspire America.”

They sit at their desks in nondescript offices, focusing on the task at hand. They do not take credit for their work; they focus on making sure quite simply that the work gets done -- that at the end of the day there is still a Work to *be* done. They train the new faces, and help the old faces with their re-entry to the world. They assure that the wheels of the world keep spinning, despite the noise that rises incessantly from that ravenous beast called "The People."

The People. Who in hell are The People, anyway? Valenti looked out toward the courtyard, which was in turn contained by the high walls of the security compound. Are we considered The People? Not by The People, he thought: they consider us the drones, the underguard, the paper pushers, tax collectors, the uniforms and faceless minions of a power that they can't identify. And yet we are doing nothing, exist for no reason, other than to serve *them.* And when someone we've put on their pedestal makes a move that gains attention, then they *LikeIt!®*. Or they don't. And 20 minutes later, they've forgotten whatever it was entirely, and are on to thinking about where to go for dinner. He turned away from the window, looking back toward work on the desk but focused on a point a few feet above it, mid-air and empty. We've finally given the people what they want. And woe unto us: they love it.

He sighed, logged off his workstation, and got up to shut the lights before heading out the door.

LikeIt!®

I, Maury Andritch, was inaugurated as Vice President of the 52 United States of America on January 20, at the ripe old age of 35. From early November the previous year until the 19th of January, I spent pretty much every waking hour immersed in what had, over three decades of fine tuning, become officially titled the Selected Federal Official Immersion Boot Camp for Training and Development ---- but everyone in the world called it the Georgetown Jamboree. With each incoming class of selectees, gaps in the program were identified, improvements and refinements were proposed and discussed by Congress, and then presented for vote (We *LikeIt!®*, the people would shout via 200 million buttons pressed simultaneously). By the time I showed up at the Jamboree for the first time, it was a well-oiled machine for producing reasonably clear-thinking and informed legislators, representatives, and leaders for the nation in the remarkably short space made available between selection and inauguration. 5:00am wake-up call (We *LikeIt!®*), and after breakfast and calisthenics, 3 hours of civics training. Coffee break. then at 10:00am, and hour of history review, and another hour of practical application governance, with a dollop of parliamentary procedure (We *LikeIt!®*). After lunch, more civics, and then two hours of direct tutoring with our assigned civil service guards. Finally the rest of the afternoon was devoted to public speaking and rhetoric (We *LikeIt!®*), and then three hours after dinner for review and study. Lights out at 11:00pm, and then we'd start again the next morning. With the exception of field trips to familiarize us with the District and the locations of all the halls of government, this was it, seven days a week.

Lou Valenti was our task master, our surrogate father, our spirit guide, missionary, and father confessor. I see now that much, if not most, of what we accomplished in those days as a governing body was due to the unseen hand of Valenti. Outside the graduates of the Jamboree, he was an unknown figure, like most career civil service officers. But he'd worked nearly from the beginning at herding the scattershot selectees of each class through our paces; he transformed us from simple people from among 'The People' into 'Those Who Lead'.

"C'mon, you clowns, up and attem! We've got a long way to go today, *Mmm*?" Every morning Valenti would start with this, to which we'd all respond

"Long way to go every day, Lou!"

And we'd be off and running. He gave the first lecture of the first day to every class; As far as I know, it hardly varied in all the years he was there. After my third term being selected at the Federal level (talk about plumber's luck -- some folks never have to bother. Me, I get three calls), I checked back to my notes. Each Jamboree had started with the same speech, word perfect. Valenti always began: "You've all been selected, and now it's time for you to represent your slice of the community. Representation is what it's all about, my friends. And some of you may have never thought about public service before, so this will be an eye-opening few months for you. And some of you maybe have thought about, and even tried to do something about it in the past. Well, let me tell you right now: you may have great ideas, but you have no idea whatsoever how to make any of them happen. Remember that: *you haven't got a clue how to make things happen*." He'd stop then, and eyeball the whole group. "If you've been through here before, you know. The only constant here is that you don't know what you're up against. Everything changes, and by the time you are done with your term of service, all the rules will have changed again. Some of 'em, with any luck, will change for the better. And if you're particularly clever, maybe you will have had something to do with it. But right now, however annoying it might be to you, you don't know jack. And what I am here to do is make sure that you leave this place a bit less incompetent than you came in.

The first rule? Listen to me, and to my staff. The only reason we exist is to make sure you succeed, and frankly, no one except me and my staff know what it will take to make you succeed. We live and die by the needs of The People, and once we let you go, if they *LikeIt!®*, then we've done our job. And if they don't, well....if they don't my children..."

"Welcome to hell on earth."

LikeIt!®

Wondering what is happening in Washington? It's all coming right at you on the screen of your LikeIt!® paddle! What do you think of the latest action on the Chinese front? LikeIt! You think the proposal from your representative has what it takes? LikeIt! How about the President's last Weekly Friendly Chat? LikeIt!
With your personal LikeIt!® paddle, you're never out of the know, and you always have a voice. Let The People be heard, and let them know you LikeIt!®

[Brought to you by Google, Inc, LiveWire, and the clever folks at the US Treasury Special Projects board; LikeIt!® is a not-for-profit public service. Patent pending.]

I moved out to the Vice-Presidential quarters in Washington a week after the inauguration; since so much of the work was now accomplished by video chat, I planned on only being there four days a week, and keeping the rest of my time back here on the coast. But I wanted it to feel like home as best I could, so I had asked Isaac and Nadav to help me move. Laura invited herself along, saying that it would be a good opportunity to have a laugh at my expense. Joe came as well. Craig and Sally thought it would be fun to come along, and had demanded to join. I met them at the station.

“Hey, Isaac! Who in hell are all these people with you?”

“Funny you should ask. I’ve been wondering that for about ten years.” He gave me a hug. “I couldn’t keep them away; you know how we are. Nadav would be here too, but Lila convinced him that winter camping in Yosemite with her and Juha would be more rewarding.”

“More prone to psychotic incidents, if you ask me.” Laura scowled as she spoke. “And anyway, the Yosemite campground is still out of range for *LikeIt!®*, and with a friend in office, where’s the fun in that?”

We were standing under the main *LikeIt!®* screen in Union Station, its constant barrage of tickers and adverts and exploding color logos like a fireworks display above our heads. I turned to Joe, who was completely engrossed in synchronizing the ticker screen on his paddle, and flipping thru the comments in order to *Like®* or *NotLike®* the activities being broadcast for representation and review. Isaac turned to me and smirked. “He’s been heads-down like that since we got on the train; I think he’s trying to single-handedly provide as much feedback as a typical township.

“Screw you, Isaac. I just want my voice heard. Besides, I’m hella smarter than a typical township. Just look at this---the representative from the 25th district in California just proposed a bill to outlaw small yappy dogs: *LikeIt!”*

"Joe, my friend, you remain a first-class ass. And you don't live in the 25th. Or anywhere near it for that matter."

"Does that matter? My voice. Shall still. Be. Heard."

Isaac suppressed a groan as best he could, and looked at Laura, and then at me. "Are we ready? Mr. Veep?"

"Sho' nuff, my fine constituents. Come help me paint the guest room!"

We walked out of the station to the curb, where my driver was waiting. As we drove slowly across the city, I explained to them what life had been like the last few weeks. They chattered among themselves, eyes dropping down to their *LikeIt!®* paddles as I spoke. It was a strange feeling, the unspoken but ever widening gulf between my old friends --- gawping at the upholstery of the car, at the crowds on the street, at, quite frankly, *me* --- and my new place in our circle. Like it or not (*LikeIt!®*), it was clear that no matter how egalitarian I might think of myself, no matter how 'of The People' this Plumber-Now-Of-High-Office might be, I was now quite suddenly drifting away from my peers, and into a new class of being. I could hear my voice droning against the sound of the car engine, and in its cadence I heard not the old familiar Maury, but more and more the echoes of an older (but far newer to me) drill sergeant: Lou Valenti.

S.B. 67 (The Corruption Reform and Treason Act)

§ Because any attempt to disrupt the principles of fair and free representation are an attack on first principles of the nation;
§ Because the disruption of effective governance is a threat to the well-being of the nation;
§ Because a key principle of representation is public hearing and debate, without subterfuge, opacity, or coercion;
§ This Congress of the United States of America resolves that:

§ 1.1 The attempt by any citizen or permanent resident to influence a government Selectee either prior to or during their term of service without full and hasty disclosure to both the civil service and the public press shall be considered a criminal offense of treason.
§ 1.1a The attempt by any non-citizen to influence a government Selectee either prior to or during their term of service without full and hasty disclosure to both the civil service and the public press shall be considered an act of terror against the government and The People of the United States.
§ 1.2 Any entity, individual, group,

organization, corporation, or committee attempting to influence a Selected government official, or their appointees, affiliates, advisors or other members of the federal government apparatus, for personal or professional gain, shall be considered in violation of this statute.
§ 1.3 Influence is to be defined as providing personal or professional gain for either the provider or recipient of influence or their representatives; modifying potential policy or governance, or the promise of said provisions in some future time period.
§ 2.1 Violations of this act will be punishable as Treason against the Federal Government of the United States, and tried in a military court of law according to the Military Code of Conduct and any other applicable law.
§ 2.2 Judgment will be made by judges impaneled by lottery, selected from the permanent civil judicial service and the armed forces judiciary.

When Joe told me his idea, I was alternately aghast, and terrified. “Dammit, Joe: you can’t be saying this! I can’t even know that you’re thinking it!”

“Oh, c’mon, Maury. Don’t get in a huff. It’s not like we’ve done anything yet. Besides, you haven’t seen this girl.” It was always a girl with Joe.

“Not done anything? Just saying what you said is a

treasonable act, Joe. For both of us! Goddammit. And I'm the Vice President! Do you know what this means?"

"Yeah---from the sound of things it looks like I'm not getting laid by the Elissa the hot corporate lawyer----"

"Joe, seriously. You would start this up just to get some?"

"Like I said, Maury: you haven't seen her. Think of the sexiest woman you ever saw, add more sexy, with huge curious eyes, and then turn her up to eleven. And make her infatuated with you."

"Joe. Listen to me: I am not. Committing treason. So you. Can have. Sex."

"What if she'd do you as well?"

"Jesus, Joe!"

"Just askin'. Sheesh." There was an awkward moment as we listened to the creaking of doors in the building. "It is actually kind of a cool idea, though. We'd make a bundle. And does anyone else really care whether a bill on corporate disclosure reform gets delayed another few months? It's a cinch to get it moving, you just need to say the word. Elissa is ready to jump when you say so."

"No. It can't happen. You know the law."

"Sure I do. But don't you think---"

"Treason, Joe. Death sentence. Not my idea of a good time. Not for you, not for me. I am not interested."

"But---"

"No buts, Joe. Please don't discuss it again." Doors swung in the silence.

"OK. Fine. I need to make a few calls. And get prepared to be jerking off for the next few months instead of entering heaven on earth with an angel named Elissa, esq."

Joe walked out into the hallway, and I sat at my desk, thinking about the plan Joe had described, and about sexy attorneys, and the small digital A/V recording device embedded in the office wall, just below the ever-present ticker of *LikeIt!*® responses from across the nation.

Depressingly, I knew what I had to do. I fired up my video link, and keyed in Lou Valenti's address.

The next time the minyan met, we were a much smaller, and subdued group. Joe, David, Craig, Sally, and Isaac were all in military prison, awaiting execution. Lila and Juha had fled the country. Laura, Nadav and I sat silently around the table, sipping tea. Not much of a minyan, just the three of us.

Apparently Joseph and Elissa were less clever than they presumed: They had been under surveillance since I had entered boot camp. The sting surrounding them had triggered the Corruption and Treason Act in full swing, and apparently I had been the last one to know about the scheme: except, of course, the public. Once the tape had been made public of my refusal to Joe, my *LikeIt!®* ratings skyrocketed (except, strangely enough, in South Carolina), and the case against Joe and his co-conspirators was pretty much a done deal. I was anything but happy about it, but my voice had little impact on any of the proceedings. I felt older than I ever had in my 35 years.

"Nadav and I are getting married." That from Laura, staring into her teacup.

"You and Nadav?" I stared at both of them sharply. "Why? I mean, Nadav, are you sure---"

"Look, Mr. Vice President, I may be gay, but I am scared and I am sad. My partner is going to be shot by a firing squad in three days, and I am under what seems to be permanent surveillance by your colleagues." He picked up a dumpling, and played with it in his fingers, avoiding Laura's glance and mine. "I don't want to be alone, and I don't want to be under suspicion. Laura's been a good friend to me, even before you two were married, and through the whole mess. It may seem to be a weird move to you, but honestly, with the climate right now, I think it's best to find safe harbor for folks like me." He dipped the dumpling in hot sesame oil, and popped it in his mouth, ending conversation again.

"'Like you'? Do you mean queer, or do you mean friends with me? You know, it's not like I asked to be Vice President. I was selected. And now I have a job and a duty and a...a moral obligation to protect and defend the constitution, and the nation, and everyone in it."

"Even Joe?" Laura, still staring into her teacup.

"Yes, even Joe. Look, Laura, do you think this has been easy for me? My best friend -- my best friend -- tried to get me to commit treason with him. I could have said yes, and then I'd be sitting right next to him, waiting for my death. Instead I did the only thing I could, the only right thing I could, and did what I did--"

"You goddammed turned in your goddammed best friend, you asshole!" The teacup dropped to the table, and her knuckles went white in clenched fists as her face turned red. "You're a shit, a vile human being, and I don't care if you are the vice president, or master of the universe, or a goddammed plumber, you've got no right to be alive when you have killed all of our friends!" She stood up, and pushed her chair away. "I'm done. Nadav, I'll be back at the apartment this afternoon." She turned without another word and walked out into the street.

I looked at Nadav, and then pulled my phone out as it began to buzz. Lou Valenti was on the other end. "We've got service guys just outside the restaurant if you need them," he said.

"You're watching all this?"

"Of course we are. Hell, you think we'd let you eat pork buns with this rabble without a full team on site? Mr. Vice President, I recommend you say something to wrap up with your friend there at the table, and join me at your office to make a public statement about the executions. With the President visiting the troops in China, you need to make your presence known right now so The People can relax and *LikeIt!®."*

I sighed, wiped my mouth, and began the next phase of my life, painfully conscious that every word, and every move, was being observed, recorded, analyzed and judged. "Nadav, I wish you both the best, and give you my blessing, for what it's worth. I think we both know that the minyan of the Pork Bun Jews is over. I don't know what happens next -- you know, it may be you next time, not me, sitting here as The People's Selected Representative -- but in the meantime, we have lives to live, and people to care for. Let's go do that." I rose and walked out the door without looking back. I wouldn't have seen anything through the tears, anyway. The two men with earpieces and dark suits met and flanked me as I reached the curb, and together we set off across town to govern the nation.

"You know," Valenti said, pacing the floor, "the executions are wildly popular. Just look at the *LikeIt!®* ratings." Turning toward the ticker with a smile.

"I know, I know. When is the President coming back from the front?"

"The day after the executions. Clever move. Maggie is a newbie to the Selected Service, just like you; but damn she is a natural. Maybe it comes from running a household with six children and two husbands. Politics isn't much different in that context..."

"All I know is that it pisses me off she gets to shake hands with the troops while I'm stuck here dealing with a pile of steaming metaphorical horse manure."

"And that is exactly what makes her a great President! Talk about maneuvering! C'mon, boy, you know you *LikeIt!®*. And has she made you brownies yet? They're to die for."

So that was the end of the minyan of the Pork Bun Jews of Pacific Street. It's hard to gather around a table when all your fellow gatherers have been rounded up and shot, or have gone underground, hiding behind false names and shifted faces in countries far from this one. I made my statement, with just the right dollop of remorse and consternation, and assured the nation that the President and I would do "everything in our power to curtail such nefarious activity, from whatever source, and whomever might be involved." My *LikeIt!*® ratings increased almost 60% overnight. In the following months, Congress passed additional legislation to strengthen the Corruption Reform and Treason Act -- they were calling it "Carta" -- and tying it to RICO II, and giving Homeland Security even more leeway in seeking out and stamping out the practices. The Homeland Undercover Surveillance teams became ubiquitous, and as my term of office wound its way through the years, we in the federal government became more effective than ever.

It wasn't more than three Selection cycles later that I received another letter from Valenti. I had been working the college lecture circuit discussing my personal history (*LikeIt!*®) to much acclaim, and was working on my second book -- *Plumbing the Workings of our Nation: What I Did, and What I Saw As Vice President* --- without much thought about Selection.

"It's like hitting the jackpot twice, eh Maury?"

"Indeed. Just like it. Too much like it. How did this happen?"

What do you mean, boy? You know how this works: your name gets drawn, and off we go."

"Lou, there are almost 350 million people in this country. How on earth does just one of them get picked twice to serve? And in the White House?"

“Careful what you say, boy. You know this call is being recorded.”

“Of course, Lou. Of course. I mean nothing by it. I will look forward to seeing you at the Jamboree.”

Of course you all know that President Andritch served a full term, helping to shepherd the nation into the beginning of the Growth Decades. I saw another state joined to the Union on my watch (*LikeIt!*®), and the appointment of more than 25 new diplomatic proconsuls to oversee our ever-growing garrisons around the globe. There was little talk of the minyan executions this time, and while there were ever more attempts to corrupt the system, through bribery, coercion, persuasion, and counter-propaganda, the DHS commandos -- Carta in hand -- were effective in preemption. And none of it reached to my office. My VP was a decent man, an accountant by trade, and together we had a pretty good run. And by this time Valenti had moved his office from across the mall to the West Wing. It made more sense, what with all the communications needed between the governing branches and the Service.

On January 20th, the day the US Presidency was permanently altered from a Selected position to a hereditary lottery, only 30 cases of champagne were consumed (its import and consumption having been severely restricted by the Foreign Tariff and Pollution Act). Nearly 900 parades were organized between the borders of Oregon in the West, and Tennessee in the East. 23,203 births were recorded in the 52 states.

11,576 deaths occurred between sunrise and sunset. Of those deaths, 485 were eventually recorded as homicides, 200 of them accidental, and not a single spousal act of passion. As house fires had become a common act of political reaction and government retaliation, none had been recorded for more than 30 months. Class action suits had been deemed unconstitutional by the Supreme Court, and more than 17 tornadoes were recorded on US territory, 9 of them in conjunction with the appearance of aliens, angels, and/or the face of Jesus on an inanimate object. On that clear, cold winter day, I walked out of Washington and onto a plane that took me not, as I had expected, back to my home in San Francisco, but to my current undisclosed location, from where I may speak --- but only under close scrutiny. And I may travel --- but only under cover of night, and only with armed escort.

I give my speeches, and I write my books, and I don't even try any longer to buck the censors. What's the point? They are my keepers, and know what I'm thinking before I do half the time. We both have had the same teacher, after all. And let's face it: he and they are still on the same side. Me, I'm not an enemy, but I'm not on the team. I'm in that wretched limbo that we no longer even acknowledge as existing in this country: how can we have political prisoners when politics is itself completely transparent, utterly egalitarian, and perfectly popular?

It was a rainy, bleak afternoon the day that I finally found the courage to ask the question that had been haunting me since my last Jamboree. This was my fourth Selection cycle, and I'd shambled through the indoctrination like a sleepwalker, knowing all the questions and all the outcomes, all the routines and all the routine surprises. The clerks from the civil service knew me now, and I was beginning to feel more of a kinship to them than to any of the others in the Jamboree class. They were newbies, freshman congressionals and newly-minted officials. I was a 3-term White House veteran. And as the rain washed over the Georgetown campus, and the selectees were all engrossed in packing their kits for the big move across town, saying their farewells and see-you-at-the-office-ha-has, I trudged across the quad to the low-lying building which housed the administrative offices, and walked through the unmarked door behind which Lou Valenti sat every afternoon of every Jamboree. I walked through the door and, without saying a word, sat across the desk from the man. I looked at him, and after a long moment, he looked up from his paperwork, and let the pen drop from his hand to the desktop. He smiled. "Hmmmm?"

"Colonel Valenti..."

He cut me off. "It's Lou, boy. We know each other too well for formalities at this point, eh? What's it you want, Hmmm? I can see the question behind your eyeballs; it's dying to jump out at me. So, go ahead and spit it out. I need to be back at the White House in an hour."

I looked directly in his eyes. "Lou, it's just...well,

really. It's not my first time around the block here, is it? And all those others, the newbies, they all think it's dumb luck that we're here together, and I got dumped in yet again..."

"And you think it isn't?" He stared into me.

"Is it?"

Valenti leaned back in his chair and folded his hands together. "They have their doubts, you know. But nothing that's big enough to matter. Besides, the gratitude gets them, and the excitement gets them, and the thrill that even a veteran like you can remember from that first time gets them. And they don't ask. But here you are, hmmm, asking."

"And?"

"And what, Maury?"

"Lou, why am I here a fourth time? Did you fix the lottery?"

A laugh started deep in his chest, and then suddenly cut off. "Is it fixed? Of course it's fixed, boy. You think I'd let just any fool lead this country? Hell, no. I love this country too much for that. Not every Selection, that would be tedious and useless. And anyway, even in the old days congress was mostly just a room full of yahoos anyway. Hell, random selection there works out just as well. But for the big guns? No way I'm letting that go. I built us back from cinders, from cinders, boy: that took a lot from me, and all of us. And now the Service is invested in keeping us moving forward. So we watch, and we plot, and we wait. And sometimes someone comes along who looks like a good person for the right time, and yeah, that's when a clever plumber gets a funny letter in the mail." He looked at me, his brow a dense thicket of wrinkles, and scowled. "Look, Mr. President. I have only one concern, and that is the continuance of this nation. It's not power, and it's not politics, and it's not appearances, and it's not the resting place of my supposedly immortal soul. I've done what I think is right, and by god, it's been working, hhmm? And I will continue in my work, and will lie, and manipulate, and fix, as long as I am able."

"Any other questions?"

I looked down at the table, biting my lip, the thoughts racing out of my head as I realized the futility of going against this force I was seeing now, for the first time, so terribly clearly. "No, Lou. No other questions. I suppose we'll be working even more closely, this coming term?"

"Like blood brothers, little plumber boy. Like blood brothers."

It's been a long road, and I've grown along the way. But now I'm tired, and I can see the end. I sit here, typing out these words, knowing full well that they will be confiscated and destroyed before they see the light of day. But know that this final statement of Maury Andritch, former President of these 53 United States, one-time plumber, first-in-minyan and last living member of the Pork Bun Jews of Pacific Street, know that this statement shall live beyond me, and beyond the insanities of our times.

There was another sighting of Trump just the other day, out on the coast; the true believers and the America Firsters and the neo-Maga Friedmanites have been streaming to the site. And the *LikeIt!®* votes have been all over the map. While I am alone here, now, I do not plan to die alone. I will be joining the burgeoning hordes, making a long-planned appearance. But when I do, it will be the last of the grand appearances of the last of the Pork Bun Jews. A joke for my long-lost friends, for Joe who would have pissed himself with glee at such a prank. For I plan to trump the archangel of the Trumpists, and have an apotheosis of my own. You think the *LikeIt!®* charts are madness now? Wait until I've done my bit. And poor old Valenti, well…Valenti will have some serious "hmmmm"-ing to do before he can regain any semblance of the status quo. At least I hope so. A new political sect is a good departing gift, I think. And maybe, just maybe -- with the help of a few apostles, a few converts from the Reaganites and the

Trumpists and the Flat Taxers and Denialists -- with just a little luck, we'll be moving back toward a better place. Toward the happy, unruly, and chaotic realm of the Bad Years; a country governed by more than the last hour's *LikeIt!*® vote and an old man in a uniform. Back to the days of openly criminal activity, where you knew what thumb you were under, and just who was profiting from it.

With a little luck.

We'll see.

www.ingramcontent.com/pod-product-compliance
Lightning Source LLC
Chambersburg PA
CBHW051402250726
48656CB00006B/2222
9781520605470